Draw Along With Sammy Sloth

T0002659

The 'Get to Know Me' series is made up of resources aimed at children with additional needs and those who support them in the classroom. Developed by child psychologist Dr Louise Lightfoot and illustrated by Catherine Hicks, the series includes activities specific to anxiety, depression and Obsessive Compulsive Disorder (OCD). This book, *Draw Along With Sammy Sloth*, is an activity-based picture book story, in which individual children are encouraged to interact with the story in a creative way – through writing, drawing, scrap booking, collage, activities etc.

Active engagement helps children to understand and process information, and aids long-term recall. It has been designed to support the individual child and encourage an empathetic and inclusive environment. In this book, we meet Sammy, a sloth who lives in a beautiful tree by the sea. The story follows Sammy as he wakes up one day to find he feels funny and strange. He can't sit still and does not feel like his usual happy and relaxed self. After pacing up and down he meets Anna the Armadillo who tells Sammy that he is silly and has no right to be sad when his life is good. Sammy hears this and feels embarrassed and ashamed of how he has been feeling. Sammy hides away until he meets a kind lizard who shows him kindness and empathy.

This book was written with children with anxiety in mind, providing an opportunity to relate to Sammy's thoughts, feelings, behaviours and experiences. However, children with a range of needs may benefit from the story. The book is written in a narrative style, so it does not use diagnostic labels and is not intended for this purpose. Instead the focus is on creating a common language which children can understand and use to make sense of how they are feeling.

A practitioner guidebook is also available (ISBN 978-0-8153-4941-9).

Dr Louise Lightfoot is an Educational and Child Psychologist working with children and young people aged 0–25. She holds a BA in Educational Studies, MEd in the Psychology of Education and doctorate in Educational and Child Psychology. Louise has worked in a variety of settings ranging from mainstream schools to secure units and psychiatric facilities, and has a special interest in working to empower at risk or 'hard to reach' groups. As a person who suffers with Ehlers Danlos, stroke and dyslexia, she has a first-hand understanding of the frustrations and difficulties that accompany a specific physical or learning difficulty. Louise currently works as an HCPC registered Independent Psychologist. If you would like to discuss working with her, please contact Louise at: louise.lightfoot@hotmail.co.uk.

Catherine Hicks is an East Yorkshire artist, illustrator, wife and mother. She spent 13 years as a Registered Veterinary Nurse before injury and chronic illnesses led to her creative hobby becoming therapy. When Catherine and Louise were introduced, it was obvious they were kindred spirits and from there the Get to Know Me Series was born.

GET TO KNOW ME SERIES

Series author: Dr Louise Lightfoot
Illustrated by: Catherine Hicks

The **'Get to Know Me'** series is a series of resources aimed at children with additional needs and the professionals who support them in the mainstream primary classroom. Each resource concentrates on a different condition and comprises of three titles, available separately.

A **traditional children's picture book** – designed to support the individual child but also to be used in whole class teaching, to encourage an empathetic and inclusive environment.

An **interactive workbook**. This is a workbook version of the story in which individual children are encouraged to interact with the story in a creative way – through writing, drawing, scrap booking, collage, activities etc. (templates and cut outs will be made available online). Children are more likely to understand and process information if they have had to actively engage with it. The workbook will aid long-term recall and increase the level of understanding.

A **practitioner guide** created for key adults (teachers, therapists and parents) by a child psychologist, with activities specific to each condition. These activities will link to the books and offer practical tools and strategies to support the child and those around them in addition to the information specific to the condition to improve understanding of a child's needs to promote empathy and acceptance.

https://www.routledge.com/Get-To-Know-Me/book-series/GKM

Books included in this series:

Set 1 Get to Know Me: Anxiety
Available as a set and individual books

Book 1
Supporting Children with Anxiety to Understand and Celebrate Difference
A Get to Know Me Workbook and Guide for Parents and Practitioners
PB 978-0-8153-4941-9
eBook 978-1-351-16492-4

Book 2
Sammy Sloth
Get to Know Me: Anxiety
PB 978-0-8153-4953-2
eBook 978-1-351-16452-8

Book 3
Draw Along With Sammy Sloth
Get to Know Me: Anxiety
PB 978-0-8153-4942-6
eBook 978-1-351-16484-9

Set 2 Get to Know Me: Depression
Available as a set and individual books

Book 1
Supporting Children with Depression to Understand and Celebrate Difference
A Get to Know Me Workbook and Guide for Parents and Practitioners
PB 978-0-8153-4943-3
eBook 978-1-351-16480-1

Book 2
Silver Matilda
Get to Know Me: Depression
PB 978-0-8153-4945-7
eBook 978-1-351-16476-4

Book 3
Draw Along With Silver Matilda
Get to Know Me: Depression
PB 978-0-8153-4946-4
eBook 978-1-351-16472-6

Set 3 Get to Know Me: OCD
Available as a set and individual books

Book 1
Supporting Children with OCD to Understand and Celebrate Difference
A Get to Know Me Workbook and Guide for Parents and Practitioners
PB 978-0-8153-4948-8
eBook 978-1-351-16468-9

Book 2
Tidy Tim
Get to Know Me: OCD
PB 978-0-8153-4950-1
eBook 978-1-351-16460-3

Book 3
Draw Along With Tidy Tim
Get to Know Me: OCD
PB 978-0-8153-4951-8
eBook 978-1-351-16456-6

DRAW
ALONG WITH SAMMY SLOTH

GET TO KNOW ME: ANXIETY

DRAW YOUR OWN PICTURES FOR THE SAMMY SLOTH STORY

DR LOUISE LIGHTFOOT

ILLUSTRATED BY CATHERINE HICKS

Routledge
Taylor & Francis Group

LONDON AND NEW YORK

First published 2020
by Routledge
2 Park Square, Milton Park, Abingdon, Oxon OX14 4RN

and by Routledge
52 Vanderbilt Avenue, New York, NY 10017

Routledge is an imprint of the Taylor & Francis Group, an informa business

British Library Cataloguing-in-Publication Data
A catalogue record for this book is available from the British Library

Library of Congress Cataloging-in-Publication Data
A catalog record has been requested for this book

ISBN: 978-0-8153-4942-6 (pbk)
ISBN: 978-1-351-16484-9 (ebk)

Typeset in Stone Informal
by Apex CoVantage, LLC

CONTENTS

WORK BOOK INSTRUCTIONS FOR PRACTITIONERS, PARENTS AND CARERS

The work book or draw along booklet can be useful in engaging children with poor literacy or a perceived dislike of formal 'work'. Often students with poor literacy, or those who struggle with comprehension, are not readily engaged in stories that may be of therapeutic value to them. Some children appear to read well but, without additional prompts, may not understand the story or how it may relate to others/themselves. Often children will read with a focus on speed rather than on understanding and will look to the pictures for information when asked questions about what they have just read.

In taking away the pictures, this forces children to be active in their engagement with the story itself as they cannot rely on images to support their understanding. By asking pupils to draw (or colour pre-drawn images dependent on ability) images that correspond to the given text, this not only consolidates their understanding of the story but helps to engage the child in a creative process. Some children are more readily engaged in a task in which they can take ownership due their participation. They are able to create their own book which can represent their abilities when applied, highlight any specific skills and act as a reminder of what they can achieve, especially if this surpasses their own expectations.

The booklet should be read with the support of a suitably skilled adult who has an understanding of the child's literacy abilities. If the child is able to read the story they should be encouraged to do so and to draw on each page a corresponding image. For able or confident pupils, they may be able to draw the complete image using pens/crayons complete with facial features depicting the mood and tone of the scene. Others may need more support and may colour, cut and stick in pre-drawn images and draw facial expressions with prompting from an adult or through choosing a facial expression from a given selection. Some children may be hesitant to draw but have great ideas and may ask an adult to draw their vision or use a computer to search for suitable images. However the book is completed, what matters is that all work is child-led and that their work is treated in a non-judgemental and positive manner. The adult should reassure the child that there is no right or wrong way to approach the task

The adult should gauge how appropriate it is to use the follow up questions provided (this may depend on verbal skills, confidence and trust/rapport) and, if appropriate, the adult may decide to explore in depth a particular section of the story, for example 'asking for help' if this is pertinent to the child's behaviour. In such a case they may decide to use the provided activities that are linked to each section of the story. An older or more able child might go through the book drawing each picture, discussing relevant topics and completing every additional activity. For some children, this process may be too much emotionally/beyond their attention span. The length of each session, the adult chosen to support the child, and timing of the session are all factors that will contribute to the success of the work.

Adults engaging in such work should be suitably supported. Best practice is to offer supervision to them by an appropriate adult in recognition of the emotionally challenging nature of this delicate and potentially stressful work. Adults are encouraged to reflect on each session and to note useful insights; for example, can the child infer the characters emotions during a scene? Can they represent this through facial expression? Body language? Use of colour? How can any such observations be supported in the future?

The child is able to keep/refer back to their book and should be encouraged to take ownership of it in order to encourage engagement and improve self-esteem.

A sloth called Sammy
Lived in a tree
In a faraway land
Overlooking the sea.

QUESTIONS: *Where do you live? Is it busy or peaceful?*

He spent happy days
Climbing up trees
Enjoying the sun
And the cool evening breeze.

QUESTION: *What do you do in your spare time?*

Sammy was happy
In his beautiful home;
He had family and friends
And was never alone.

Then one morning he woke
Feeling all funny,
With ants in his pants
And a knot in his tummy.

QUESTIONS: *What did he feel like was in his tummy? Have you ever had this?*

He couldn't keep still,
Like he drank too much pop,
Thoughts rushed round his head
And they just wouldn't stop!

QUESTION: *What thoughts rush around your head?*

He felt whizzy and fizzy
And tizzy inside,
And he couldn't relax
Though he really tried.

QUESTION: How do you relax?

So he paced up and down
Till it made his feet ache,
But he didn't feel tired
He felt wide awake.

QUESTIONS: Do you have trouble sleeping? What helps?

So he climbed down the tree
And sat on a stone.
"Get off me!" he heard.
He wasn't alone.

He'd found Anna the Armadillo,
He'd sat down on her shell.
"I'm sorry" said Sammy
"I don't feel too well."

"Whatever's the matter
Why can't you sit still?
Watching you pace
Is making me ill!

QUESTIONS: *Is Anna kind? Do you think she understands
what he is going through?*

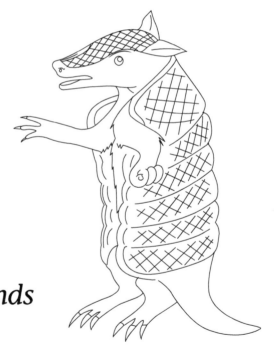

"I thought sloths were slow,
They don't rush around,
They're still and they chill
And they generally lounge"

"I was slow," said Sammy.
"But there was a change
And now I feel buzzy
And fuzzy and strange."

"You must know what's wrong,
So fix it today.
So stop with the worry
And you'll be ok."

"But that's just the problem,
I don't really know.
Nothing has happened
for my worries to grow."

Anna looked puzzled.
"That sounds silly to me.
You have plenty to eat
And your very own tree.

"You have family and friends
And a place to belong;
And you lie in sun
So what could be wrong?"

QUESTIONS: *What advice did she give her? What advice would you offer Sammy?*

Then Sammy felt silly,
As that was all true.
And shame filled his heart
What was he to do?

QUESTION: *Why do you think Sammy felt shame?*

So he climbed up the tree
And tried to forget
The knot in his tummy
That was making him fret.

And he tried to sit still
But more thoughts
whizzed about.
"But everything's fine!"
He heard himself shout.

"If you don't mind me saying,
Things don't look fine.
The fact you're shouting
Is not a good sign."

QUESTIONS: How would people know you weren't fine? Would you shout? Cry? Throw things?

Livy the Lizard
Had heard Sammy shout.
"It's ok to be mad
Just let it out!"

QUESTION: How do you let it out?

"But that's just the problem,"
Sammy replied.
"I just can't calm down
I can't stop the wiggly feelings inside.

"And Anna was right,
I've a wonderful life,
And so many others
Face hardship and strife."

"Don't listen to her,
It's ok to feel worry,
Or wobbly and bobbly
Like your minds in a hurry.

"And sometimes our worries
Are big or they're small
But sometimes we worry
For no reason at all.

"We might have a problem
The needs to be solved
And this can upset us
Until it's resolved.

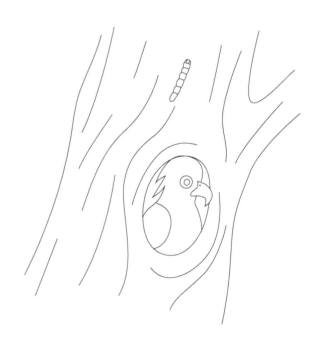

"And sometimes the small things
We worry about
Can build up and up
Until it they burst out!

QUESTION: *What can this look like?*

"And sometimes for reasons
We cannot explain,
We feel different inside
Although things look the same.

"But whatever the reason
You must never feel shame
Or guilty or silly
Or that you are to blame.

"What you need is a friend
To help you find out
What makes you feel better
And be there throughout.

"And whatever that is
We can do it together.
And remember these feelings
Won't last forever.

"I'm happy to listen
If you want to talk
Or I'll sit beside you
Or go for a walk.

"I don't know your troubles
Or why they have grown,
But I know you no longer
Must face them alone."

QUESTION: *What does Livy say to make Sammy feel better?*

Colour, cut and stick pictures – use these however you like!

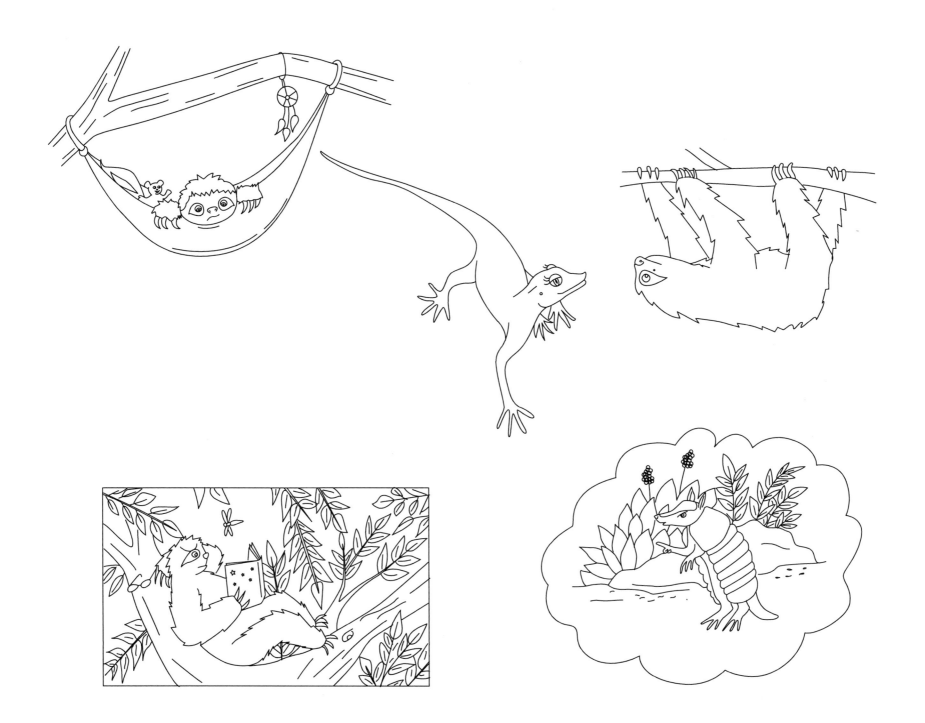